D1605306

TRADITIONS AND CELEBRATIONS

DÍA DE LOS MUERTOS

by Alicia Salazar

PEBBLE
a capstone imprint

Pebble Explore is published by Pebble, an imprint of Capstone.
1710 Roe Crest Drive
North Mankato, Minnesota 56003
www.capstonepub.com

Library of Congress Cataloging-in-Publication Data
Names: Salazar Pino, M. Alicia, author.
Title: Día de los Muertos / Alicia Salazar.
Description: North Mankato : Pebble Explore, An Imprint of Capstone, [2022] | Series: Traditions and celebrations | Includes bibliographical references and index. | Audience: Ages 5-8 | Audience: Grades K-1 | Summary: "Día de los Muertos is a special holiday to remember and celebrate loved ones. It is a Mexican tradition held to honor those who have died. Some people dress up and go to parades. Others sing, dance, and eat special food. Others decorate altars with flowers and make offerings. Readers will discover how a shared holiday can have multiple traditions and be celebrated in all sorts of ways"— Provided by publisher.
Identifiers: LCCN 2021012663 (print) | LCCN 2021012664 (ebook) | ISBN 9781663908278 (hardcover) | ISBN 9781663920881 (paperback) | ISBN 9781663908247 (pdf) | ISBN 9781663908261 (kindle edition)
Subjects: LCSH: All Souls' Day—Juvenile literature.
Classification: LCC GT4995.A4 S23 2022 (print) | LCC GT4995.A4 (ebook) | DDC 394.266—dc23
LC record available at https://lccn.loc.gov/2021012663
LC ebook record available at https://lccn.loc.gov/2021012664

Image Credits
Alamy: Jan Sochor, 13, Nacho Calonge, 29; Shutterstock: AGCuesta, 22, Auribe, Cover, 27, betto rodrigues, 1, Jareth Ley, 23, Joe Giampaoli, 17, Kobby Dagan, 5, Loes Kieboom, 7, 15, M Yerman, 12, mark reinstein, 19, Mille HL, 28, nobito, 9, Oleg Elkov, 11, Paullina Sonntag, 24, Quetzalcoatl1, 21, robert gibson z, 8, Roberto Michel, 16

Artistic elements: Shutterstock: Rafal Kulik

Editorial Credits
Editor: Erika L. Shores; Designer: Dina Her; Media Researcher: Jo Miller; Production Specialist: Tori Abraham

All internet sites appearing in back matter were available and accurate when this book was sent to press.

TABLE OF CONTENTS

Words in **bold** are in the glossary.

WHAT IS DÍA DE LOS MUERTOS?

Maria and her grandmother walk to the **cemetery**. They live in a town in Mexico. It is November 1. They visit the graves of family members who have passed away. They clean away dirt and leaves from the graves. They add fresh flowers to the graves. In the evening, they join family members for a meal.

They are celebrating Día de los Muertos. In English it means Day of the Dead.

Maria and her family spend the evening together. They might even stay at the cemetery all night. They gather to celebrate the lives of their dead relatives.

Families play music and dance. Young and old also take part in a **procession**. They carry lit candles and walk through the streets. Some people believe the candles help the **spirits** of the dead find their way to their families.

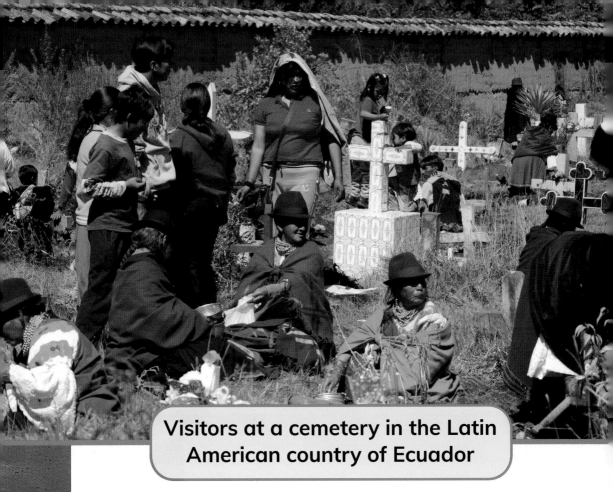

Visitors at a cemetery in the Latin American country of Ecuador

Día de los Muertos is two days long. It began in Mexico. Many other Latin American countries also celebrate it. The first day is for remembering children who have passed away. The second day is for remembering adult family members who have died.

People believe that on these two days the spirits of the dead leave the spirit world. The spirits visit their living relatives. The loved ones' spirits are able to join families in the cemetery or in their homes. They eat and dance together.

WHEN IS DÍA DE LOS MUERTOS?

Día de los Muertos is the first two days of November. It is close to Halloween. But it is not related to Halloween in any way. Some people might dress up as skeletons. The purpose of the holiday is not to dress in costume, though. It is a day to pray and remember lost family members.

The skeletons seen on Día de los Muertos are not meant to be scary. They remind people that the dead are still family even if they are in the spirit world.

Many Mexicans follow the teachings of the **Roman Catholic** Church. On the Catholic calendar, November 1 is All **Saints**' Day. November 2 is All Souls' Day. All Saints' Day celebrates saints of the Catholic Church. People pray for the dead on All Souls' Day.

A priest leads a Catholic service.

Many Mexicans also honor traditions from their **native heritage**. Día de los Muertos mixes Roman Catholic and native traditions. It is common for people to go to church or say a **rosary** for Día de los Muertos.

IN MEXICO

Maria and her grandmother set up an ofrenda at their home. An ofrenda is an **altar** with photos of loved ones who have died.

People often add food or other things that the person loved to the altar. Maria and her grandmother add lots of flowers to their ofrenda.

an ofrenda for Día de los Muertos

Until recently, celebrations in Mexico mostly involved simple family gatherings. Each family would set up an ofrenda. They would go to church to pray. The family would then go to the cemetery to celebrate.

A big display of ofrendas at Universidad Nacional Autonoma de Mexico

Today's celebrations have grown bigger. Towns and cities put up decorations. Mexico City has a parade every year. People dress up and dance in the parade. Universidad Nacional Autonoma de Mexico (UNAM) has a large display of ofrendas.

IN THE UNITED STATES

Mexicans who moved to the United States brought their traditions with them. Día de los Muertos is one of them. In the U.S., people call the holiday the Day of the Dead.

Many Mexican Americans and their children celebrate the way their families did in Mexico. They have an ofrenda, say prayers, and visit the cemetery.

Some Americans who do not have Mexican roots also join in. They might dress up and celebrate with food and music. They remember loved ones who have died.

SYMBOLS

CATRINAS

Women dress up as La Catrina. In Spanish, the word catrín or catrina means well-dressed man or woman. The Día de los Muertos La Catrina is different. She is a skeleton in a fancy dress. Women put on makeup to look like a skull. They wear traditional dresses.

Catrinas are usually women. But men can dress up too. Men wear skeleton masks with **mariachi** costumes.

CALACAS AND CALAVERAS

In Spanish, calacas and calaveras mean skeletons and skulls. Artists make calacas out of **papier-mache**. They pose them in fun positions. Some are dancing. Some are playing music or getting married.

calacas

calaveras

Calaveras are a famous symbol of Día de los Muertos. Bakers make skulls out of sugar or chocolate. People buy them to place on their ofrendas. The names of their loved ones are on calaveras. Some people give them as gifts or use them as decorations.

MARIGOLDS

Marigolds are known as flor de muerto. In English that is "flower of the dead." Marigolds are an important part of the ofrenda. Their scent is said to bring the dead to the altars. When spirits come back to find the living, the marigold scent helps them get to the right place.

VELAS DE CEBO

Velas de cebo means "candles made of fat." They are made the way Mexicans made them long ago. The candles are meant to light the path for the returning souls of the dead. People carry them during prayers and processions at midnight between November 1 and 2.

PAN DE MUERTO

Pan de muerto, or "bread of the dead," is a sweet, round loaf. It has four strips that look like bones. The bread is placed on altars. It is food for the souls of the dead who return home November 1. The next day, the living family enjoys the bread.

Día de los Muertos is an important holiday. It connects people to their heritage as well as to their Catholic beliefs. People remember and celebrate loved ones who have died. It also reminds the living to honor each day they are alive.

GLOSSARY

altar (AWL-tuhr)—a platform or table used as a center of worship

cemetery (SEM-uh-ter-ee)—a place where dead people are buried

heritage (HER-uh-tij)—history and traditions handed down from the past

mariachi (mah-ree-AH-chee)—a Mexican street band

native (NAY-tiv)—people who originally lived in a certain place

papier-mache (PAY-pur-ma-SHAY)—paper pulp with glue that makes a light material used for shaping and molding things

procession (pro-SEH-shun)—a group of people moving in an orderly way

Roman Catholic (ROH-muhn KATH-lik)—the Christian church led by the Pope

rosary (ROE-suh-ree)—a set of Roman Catholic prayers that are repeated in a specific order

saint (SAYNT)—a person honored by the Catholic church for his or her holiness

spirit (SPEER-it)—the invisible part of a person that contains thoughts and feelings; some people believe the spirit leaves the body after death

READ MORE

Eliot, Hannah. *Día de los Muertos*. New York: Little Simon, an imprint of Simon & Schuster Children's Publishing Division, 2018.

Murray, Julie. *Day of the Dead*. Minneapolis: Abdo Kids, a division of ABDO, 2018.

Orgullo, Marisa. *Celebrating Day of the Dead!* New York: PowerKids Press, 2019.

INTERNET SITES

Day of the Dead
kids.nationalgeographic.com/explore/celebrations/day-of-the-dead/

Five Facts about Día de los Muertos
si.edu/stories/5-facts-about-dia-de-los-muertos-day-dead

INDEX